CHRISTMAS
GLASGOW

Kipper Williams

AMBERLEY

A number of these cartoons originally appeared in the Guardian, *the* Spectator, *the* Sunday Times, Private Eye, Country Life *or* Recharge, *so thanks to all concerned for allowing them to be used again here. Thanks also to E&T magazine for permission to reuse the cartoons on pages 4 and 14. Cartoons on pages 7, 15, 27 and 45 © Paperlink 2016.*

First published 2016

Amberley Publishing
The Hill, Stroud,
Gloucestershire, GL5 4EP
www.amberley-books.com

Copyright © Kipper Williams, 2016

The right of Kipper Williams to be identified as the Author of this work has been asserted in accordance with the Copyrights, Designs and Patents Act 1988.

ISBN 978 1 4456 6358 6 (print)
ISBN 978 1 4456 6359 3 (ebook)

All rights reserved. No part of this book may be reprinted or reproduced or utilised in any form or by any electronic, mechanical or other means, now known or hereafter invented, including photocopying and recording, or in any information storage or retrieval system, without the permission in writing from the Publishers.

British Library Cataloguing in Publication Data.
A catalogue record for this book is available from the British Library.

Typesetting and Origination by Amberley Publishing.
Printed in the UK.

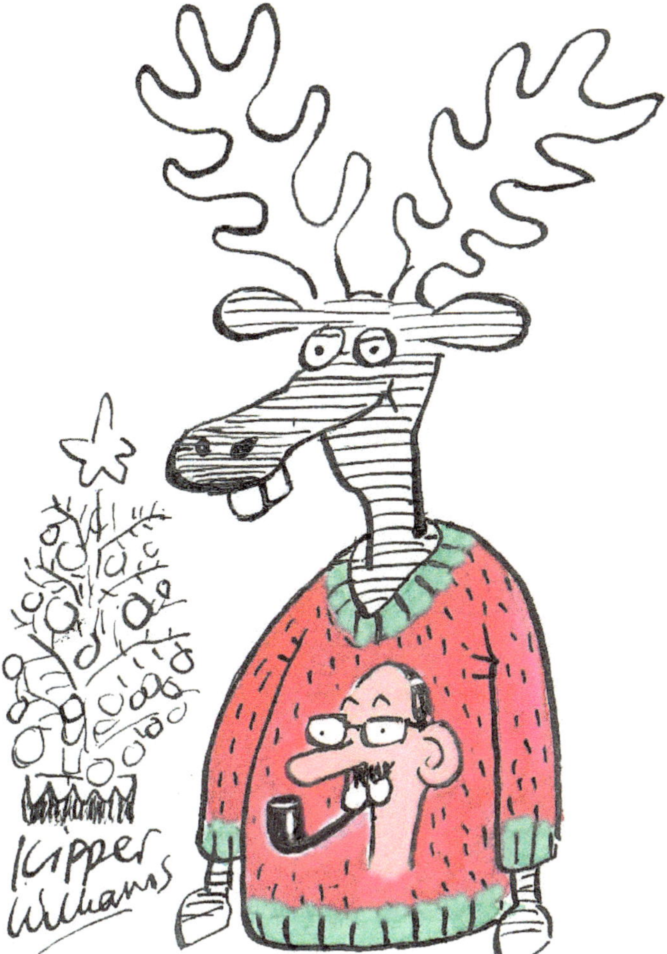
Kipper Williams

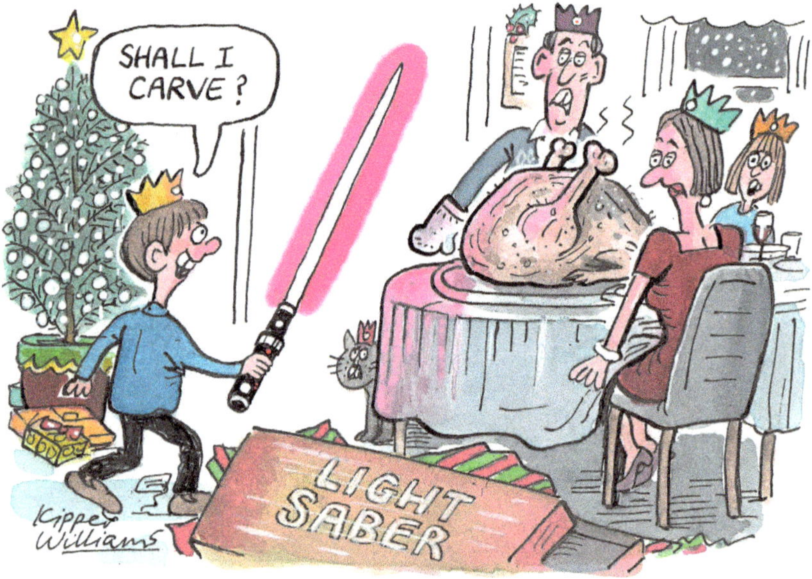
SHALL I CARVE?
LIGHT SABER
Kipper Williams

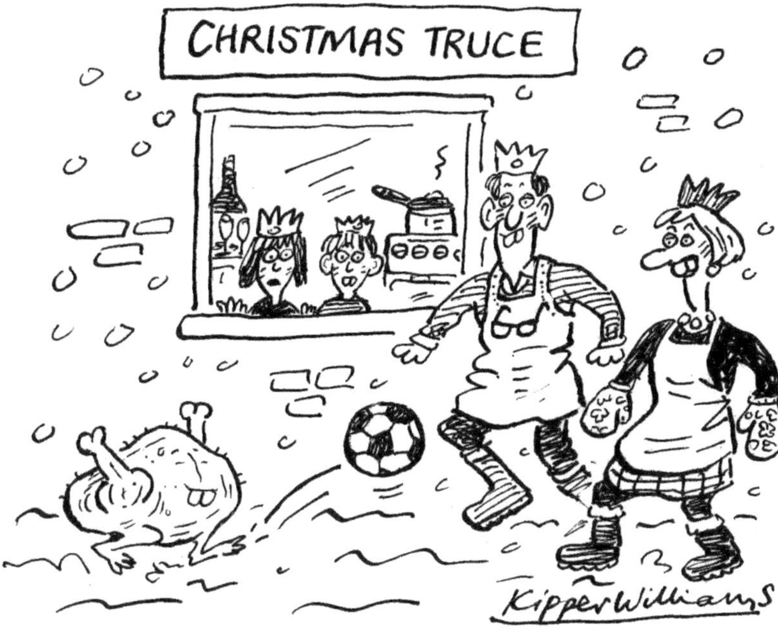
CHRISTMAS TRUCE
KipperWilliams

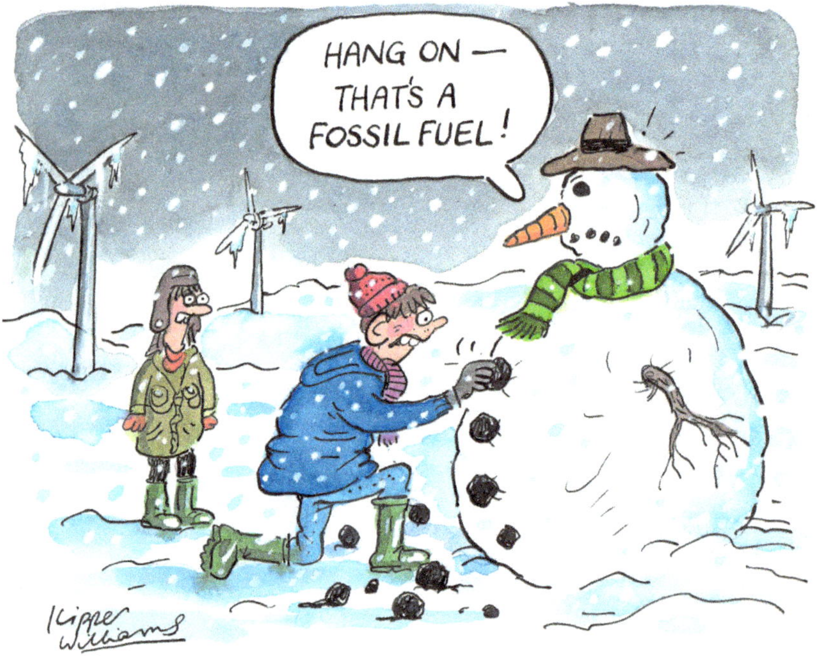
HANG ON —
THAT'S A
FOSSIL FUEL!
Kipper Williams

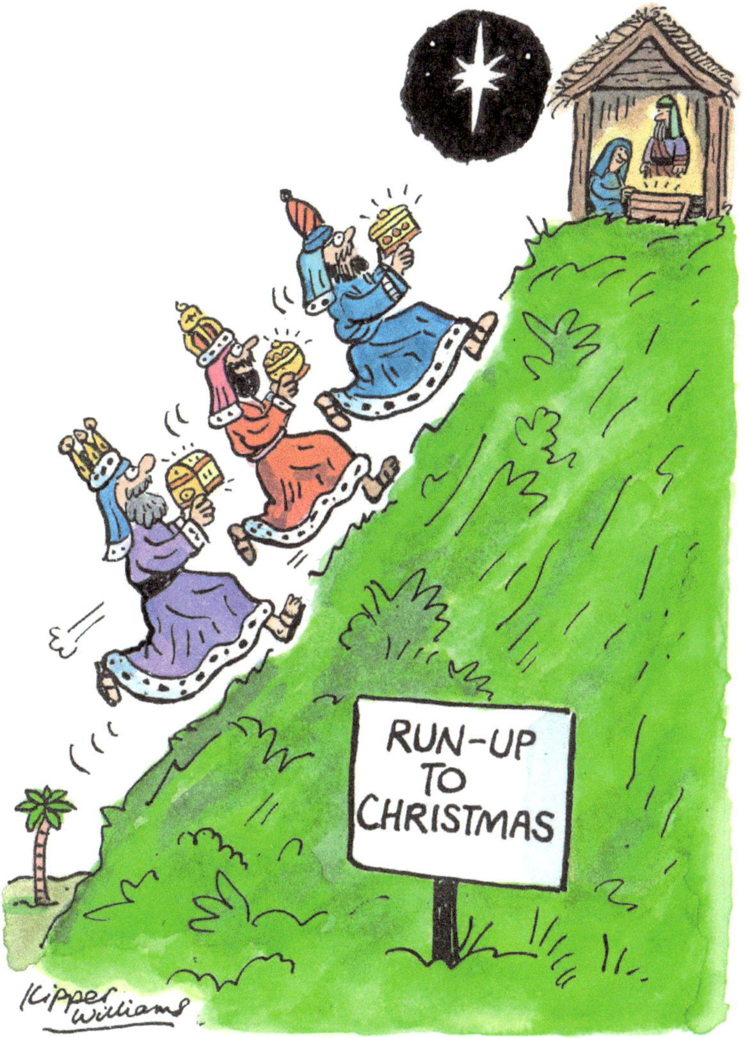
RUN-UP
TO
CHRISTMAS
Kipper Williams

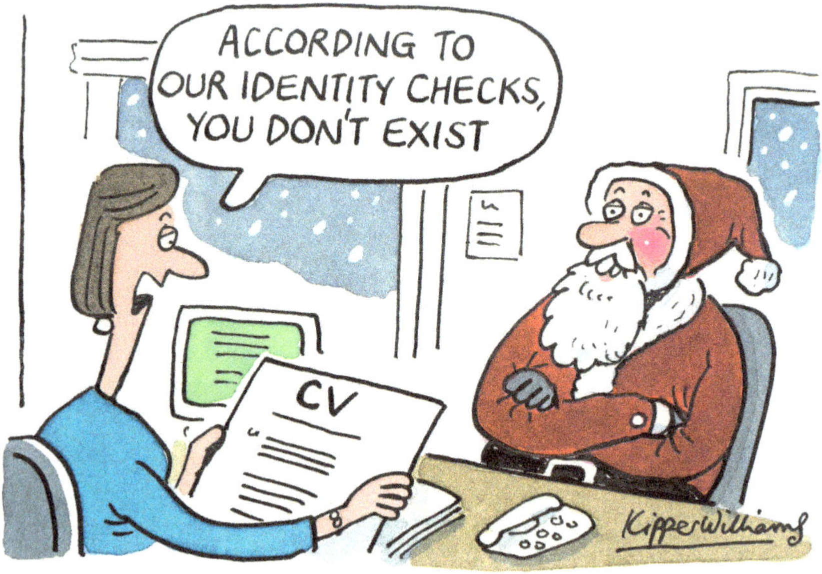
ACCORDING TO OUR IDENTITY CHECKS, YOU DON'T EXIST
CV
KipperWilliams

GOLD ! WOW !
IT WAS TRADING AT AROUND $870 THIS WEEK — BUT SOME SAY IT'LL CLIMB TO $2,000 AN OUNCE ...
AT THIS RATE WE'LL BE ABLE TO AFFORD A HOTEL

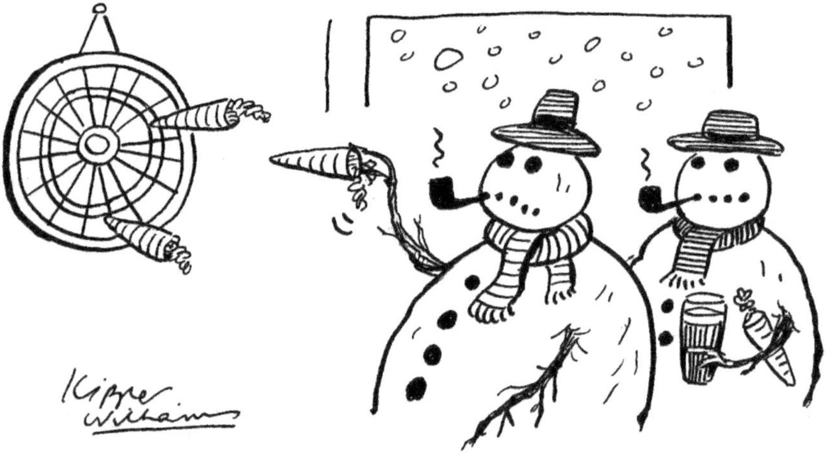
Kipper Williams

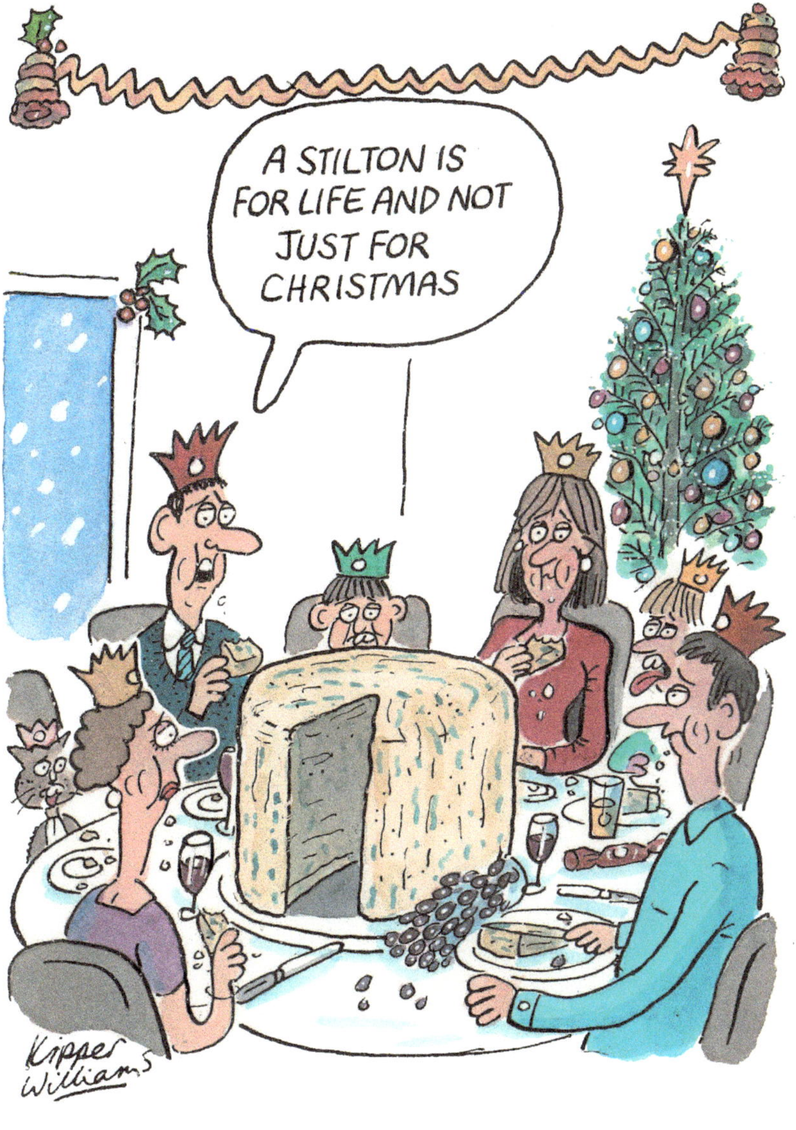
A STILTON IS FOR LIFE AND NOT JUST FOR CHRISTMAS
Kipper Williams

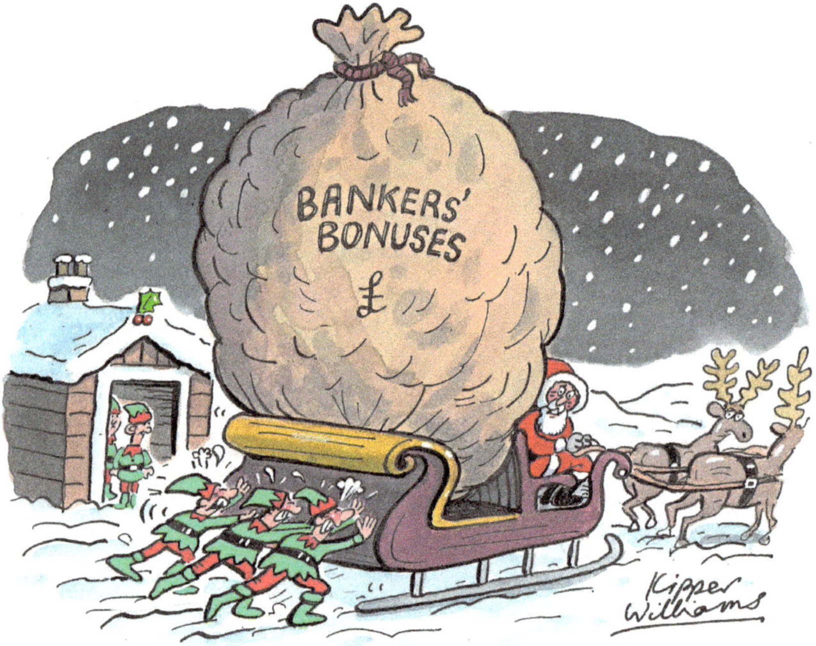
BANKERS'
BONUSES
£
Kipper
Williams

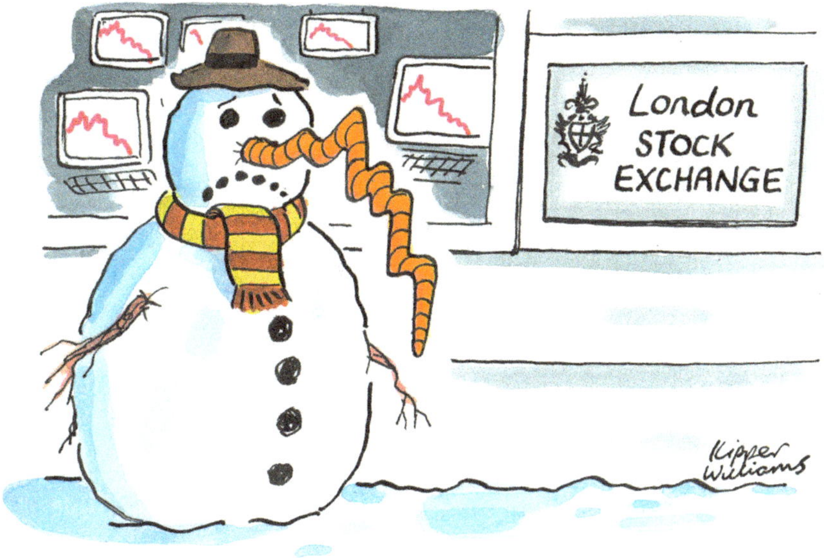
London
STOCK
EXCHANGE
Kipper
Williams

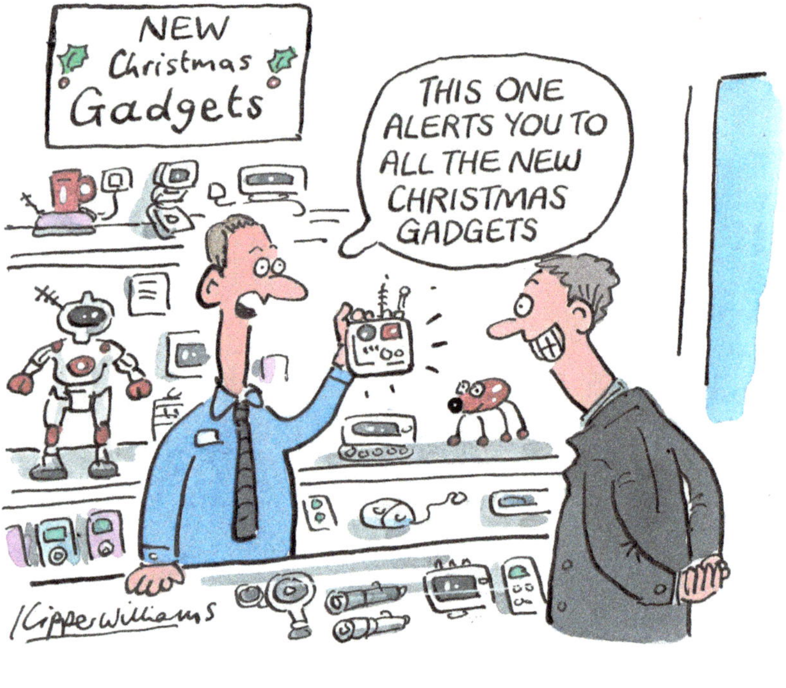
NEW Christmas Gadgets
THIS ONE ALERTS YOU TO ALL THE NEW CHRISTMAS GADGETS
KipperWilliams

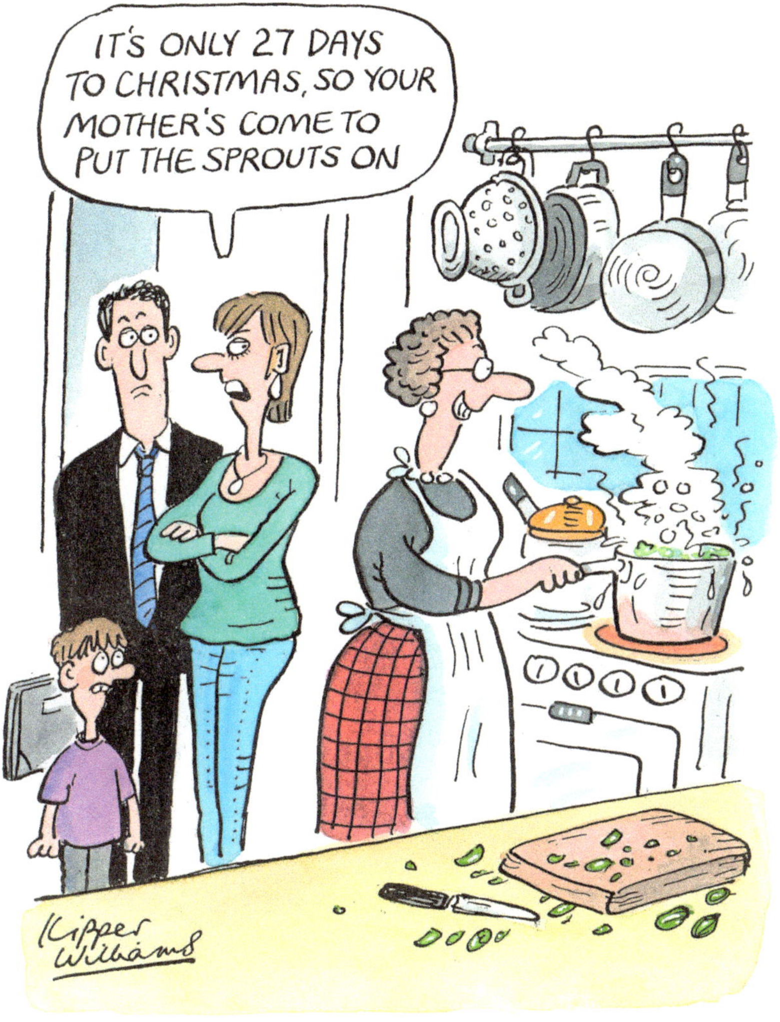
IT'S ONLY 27 DAYS TO CHRISTMAS, SO YOUR MOTHER'S COME TO PUT THE SPROUTS ON
Kipper Williams

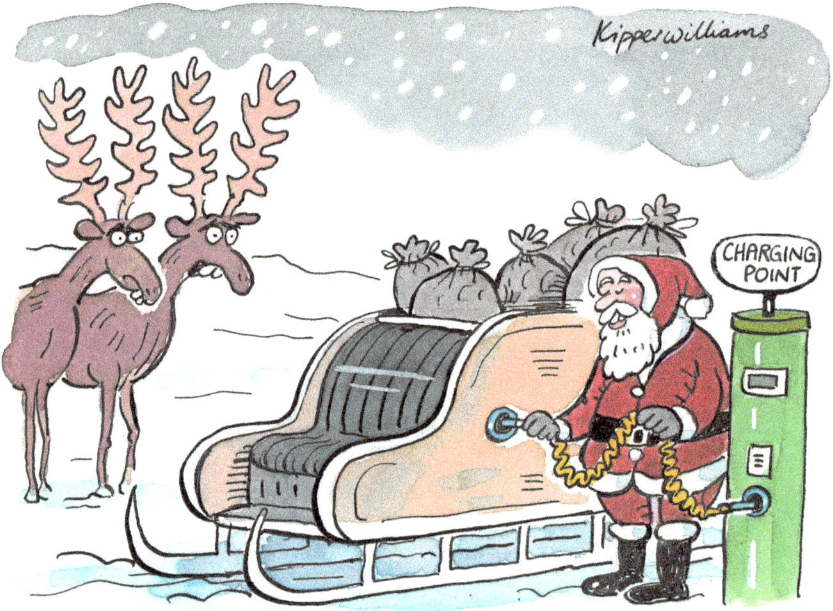
Kipperwilliams
CHARGING POINT

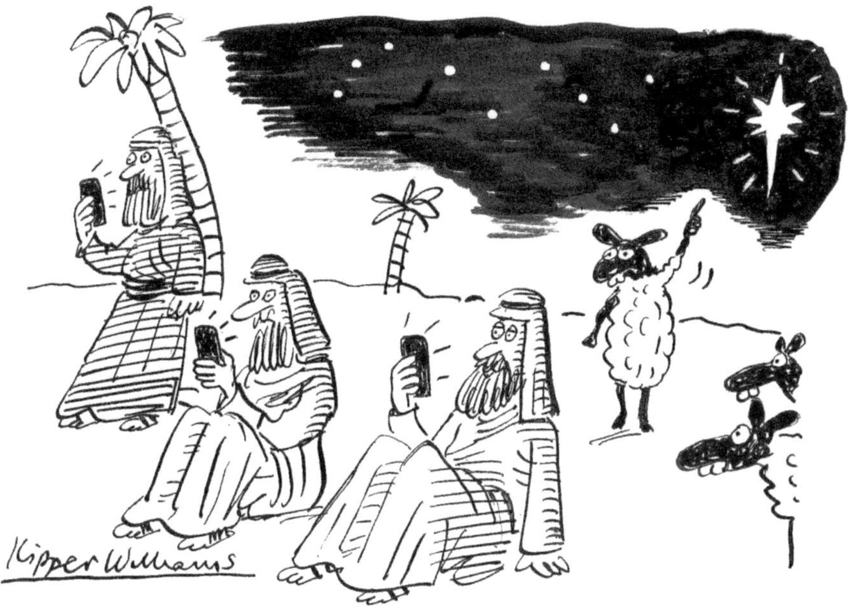
Kipper Williams

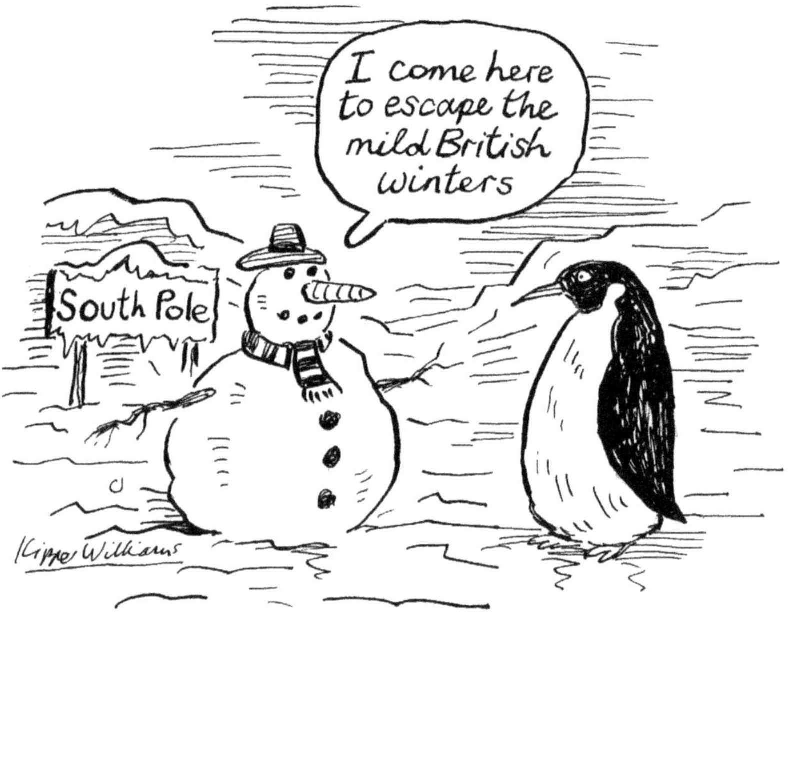
I come here to escape the mild British winters
South Pole
Kipper Williams

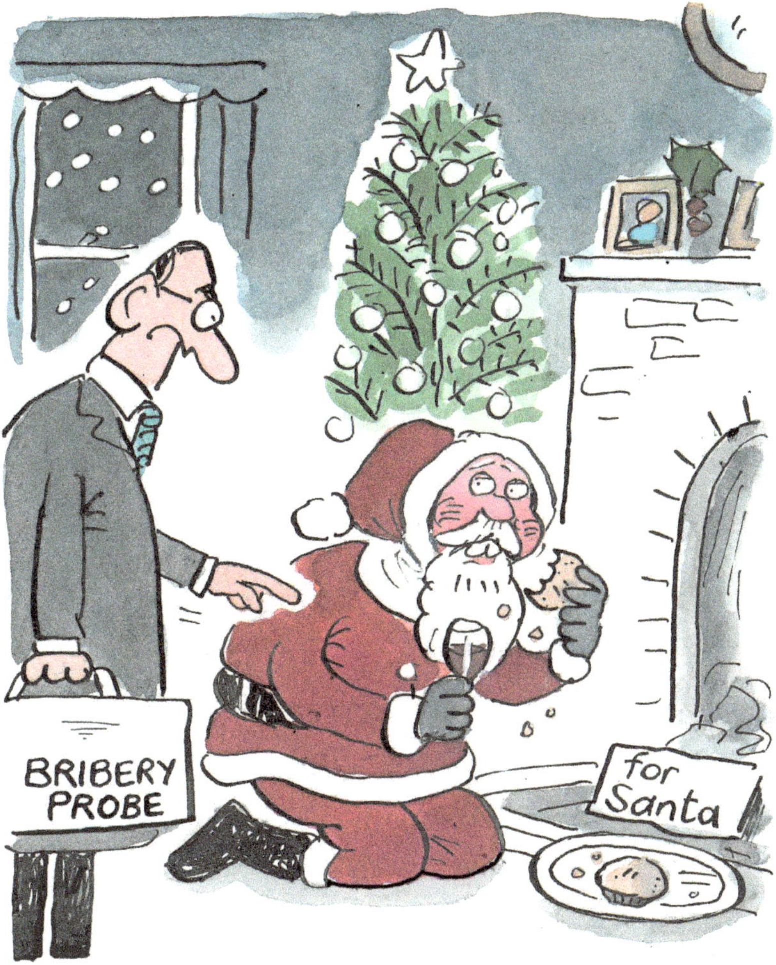
BRIBERY PROBE
for Santa

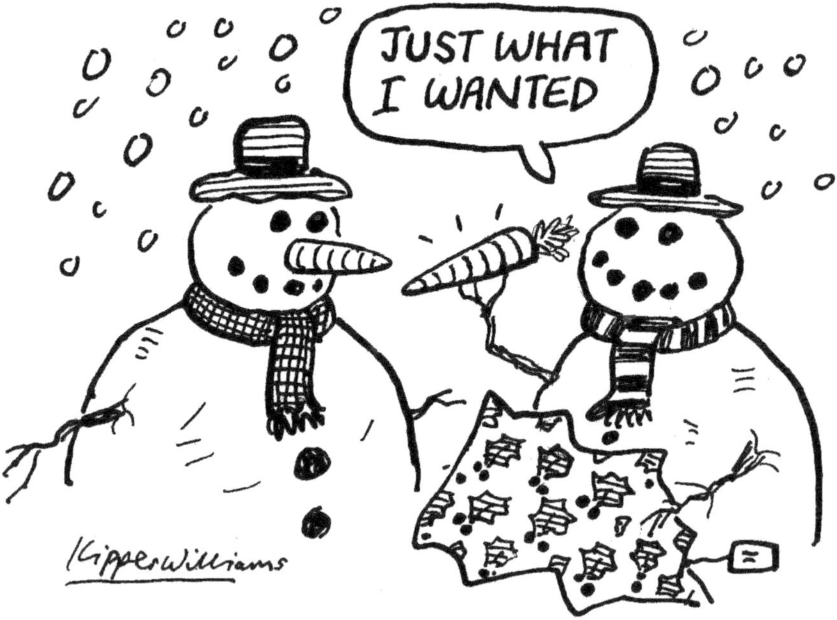
JUST WHAT I WANTED
KipperWilliams

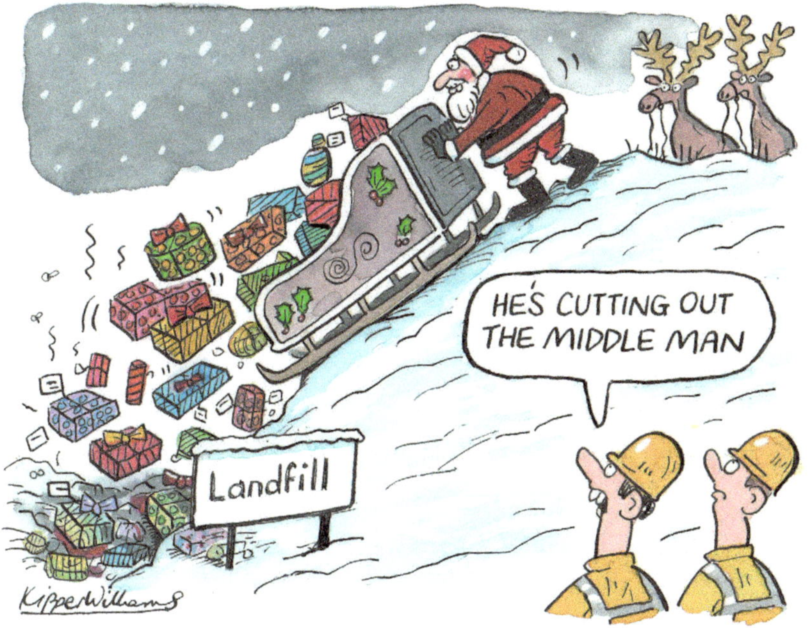
HE'S CUTTING OUT THE MIDDLE MAN
Landfill
KipperWilliams

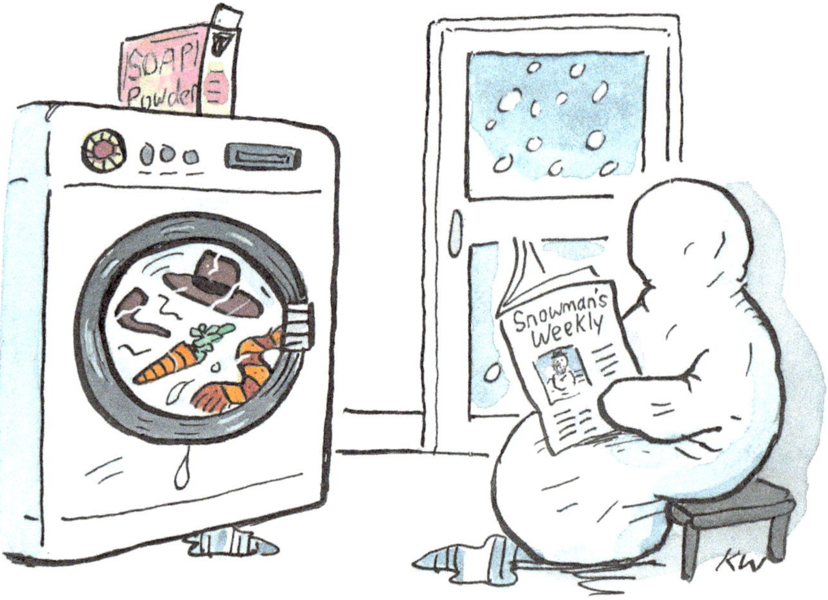
SOAP
Powder
Snowman's
Weekly
KW

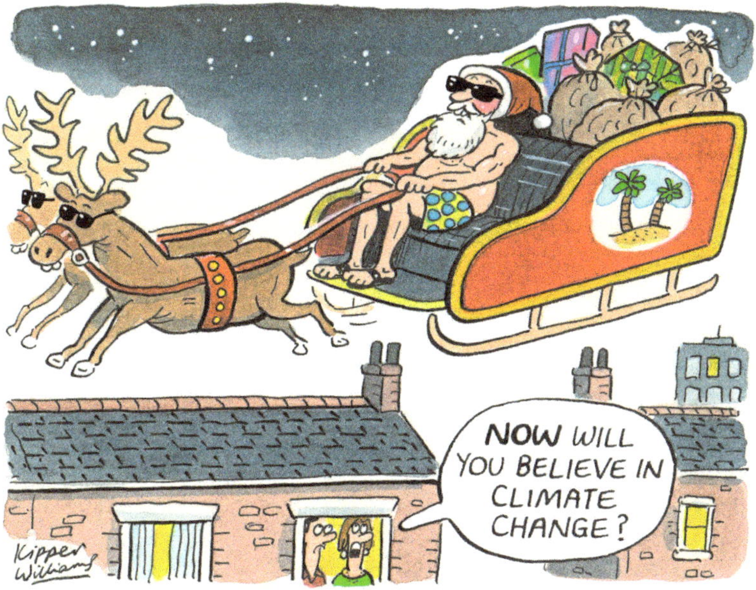
NOW WILL YOU BELIEVE IN CLIMATE CHANGE?
Kipper Williams

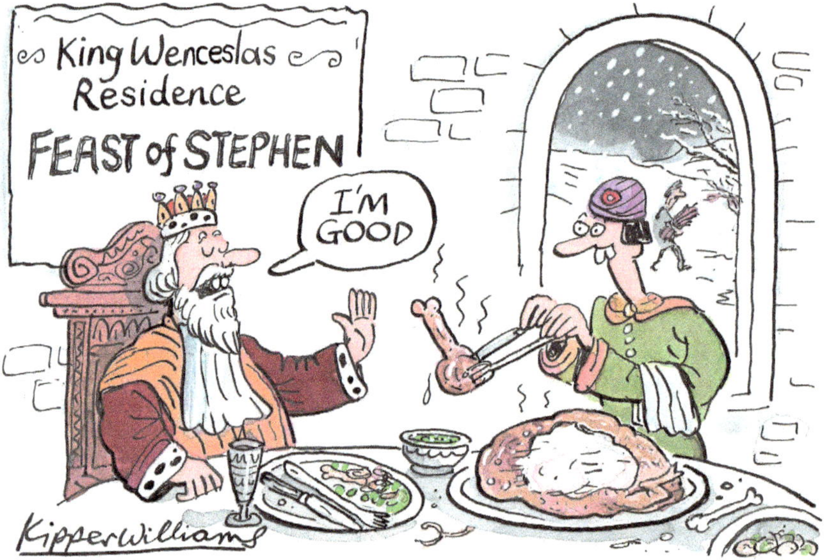
King Wenceslas Residence
FEAST of STEPHEN
I'M GOOD
KipperWilliams

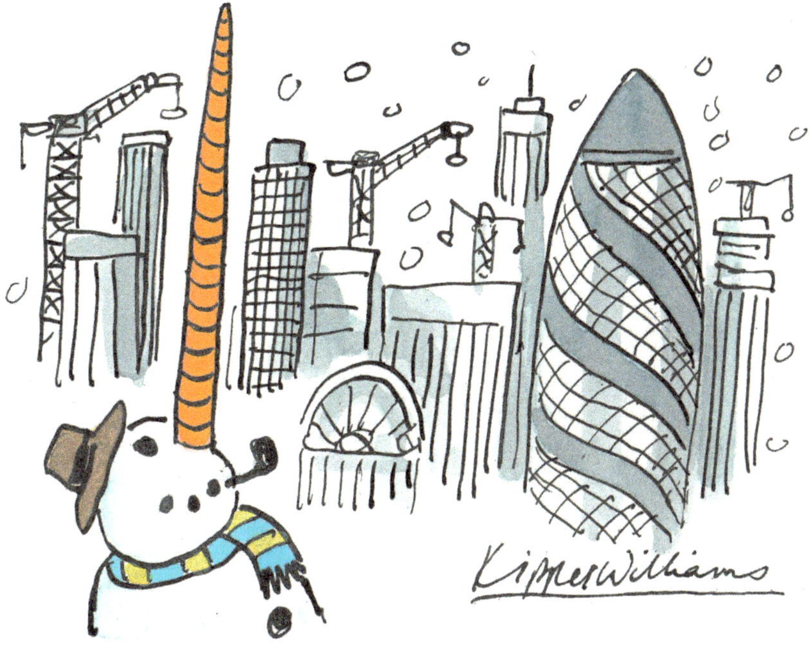
KipperWilliams

Gallery of SURREALISM
Kipper Williams

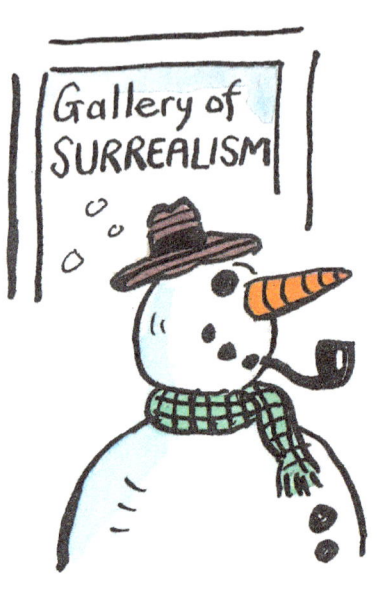

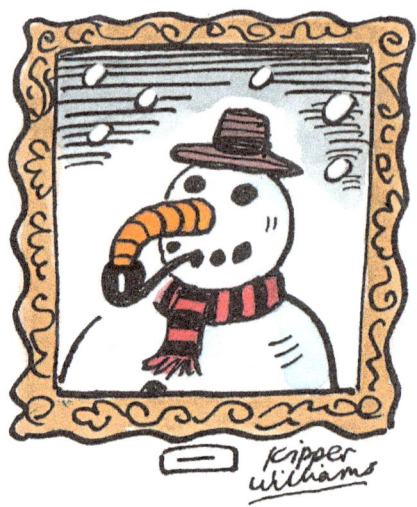

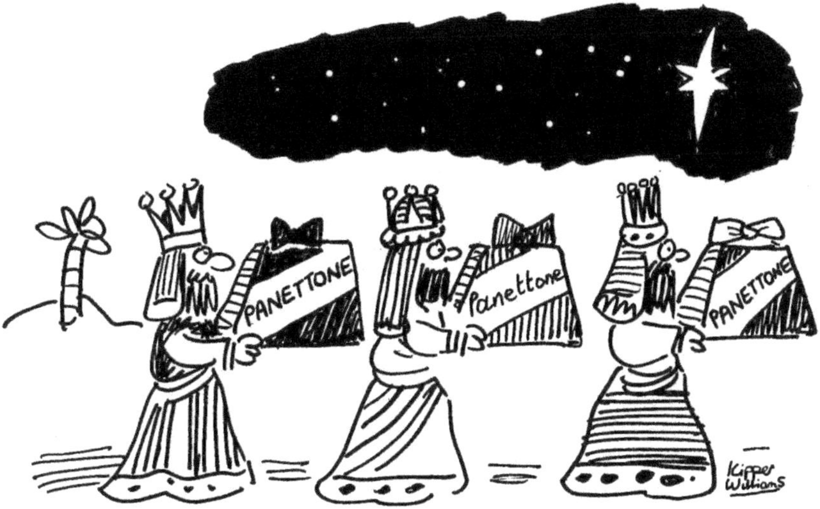
PANETTONE
Panettone
PANETTONE
Kipper Williams

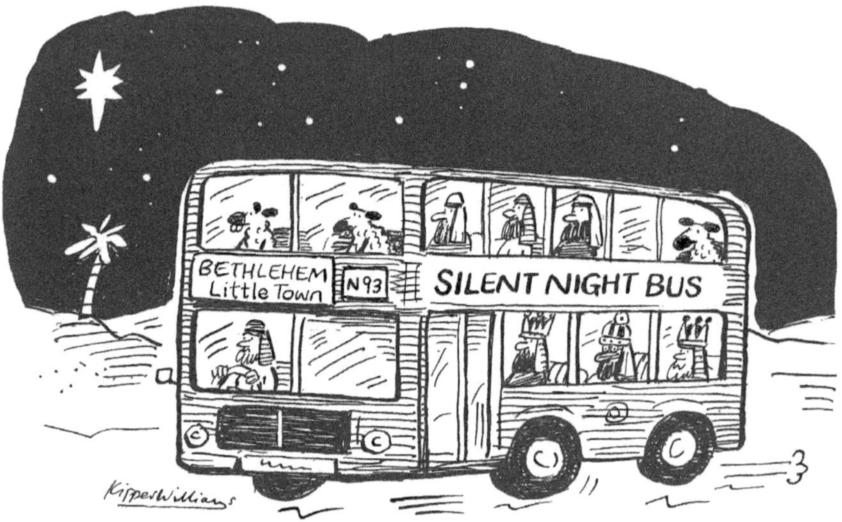
BETHLEHEM
Little Town
N93
SILENT NIGHT BUS
KipperWilliams

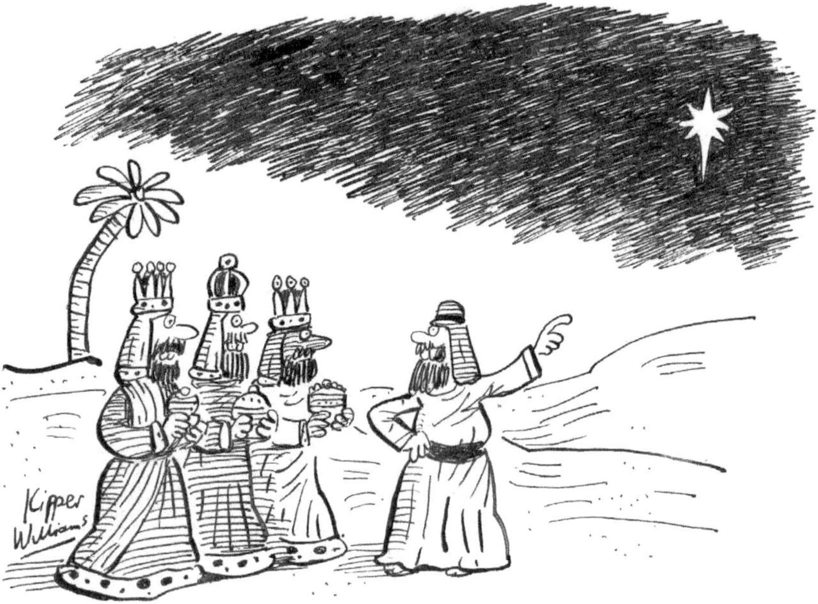
Kipper Williams

'Across the field, left at the fountain,
over the moor and right at the mountain.'

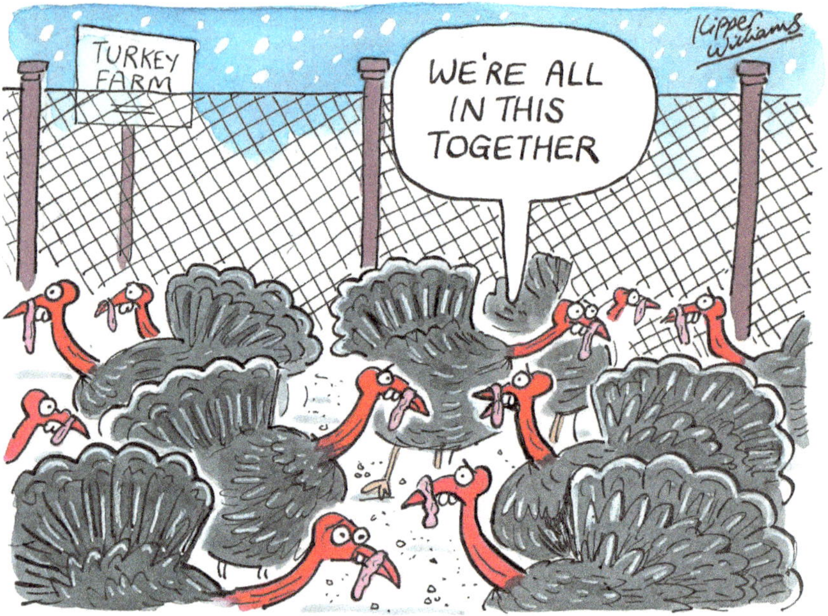
TURKEY FARM
WE'RE ALL IN THIS TOGETHER
Kipper Williams

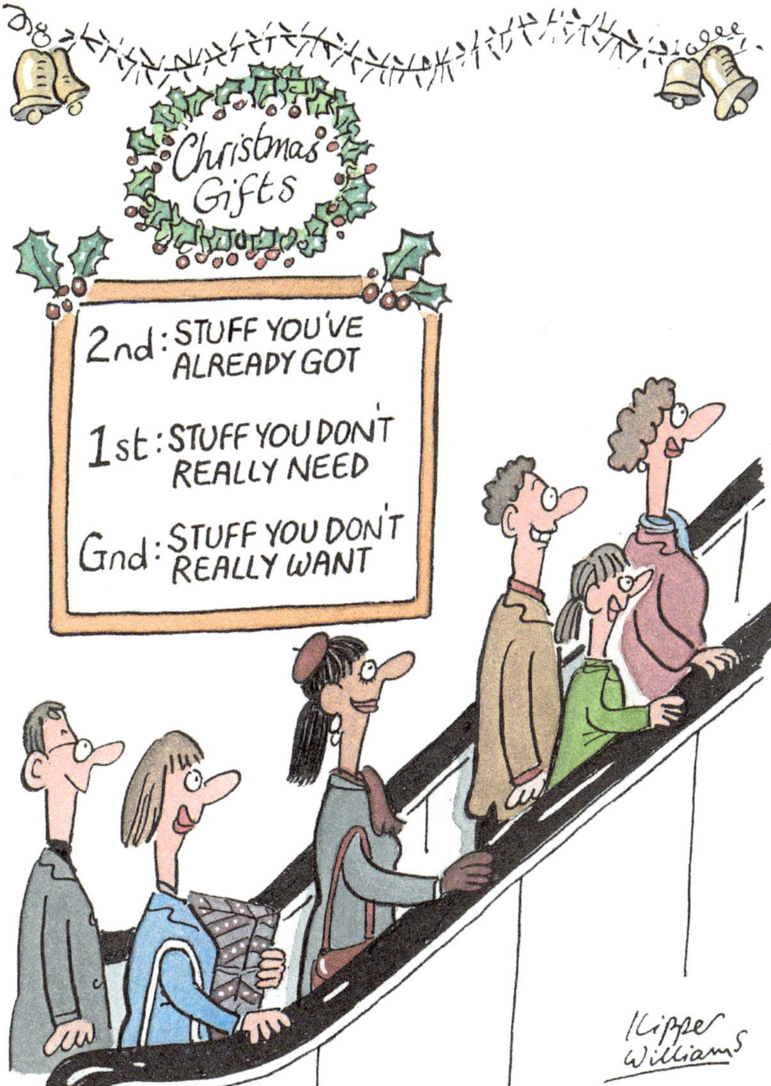

Christmas Gifts
2nd: STUFF YOU'VE ALREADY GOT
1st: STUFF YOU DON'T REALLY NEED
Gnd: STUFF YOU DON'T REALLY WANT
Kipper Williams

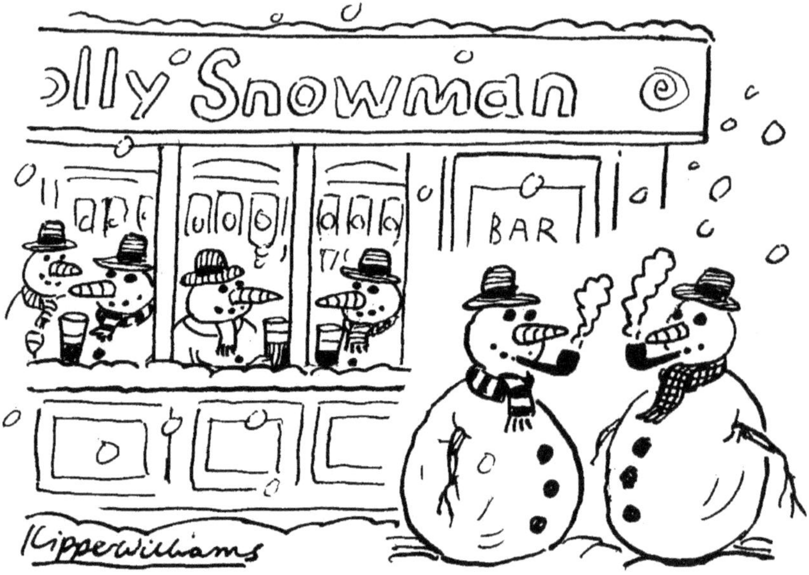

olly Snowman
BAR
KipperWilliams

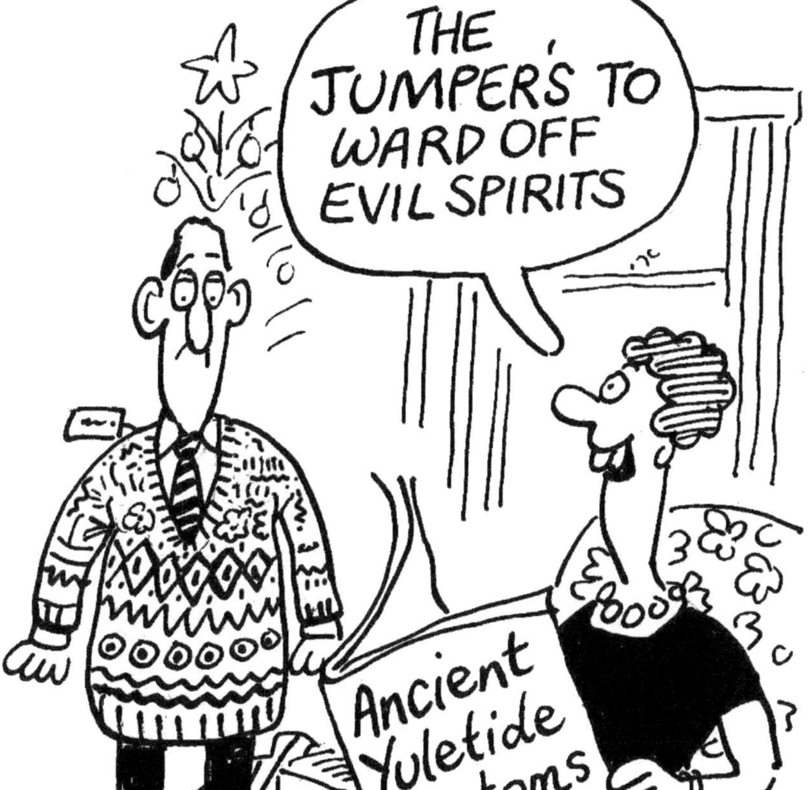
THE JUMPER'S TO WARD OFF EVIL SPIRITS
Ancient Yuletide Customs

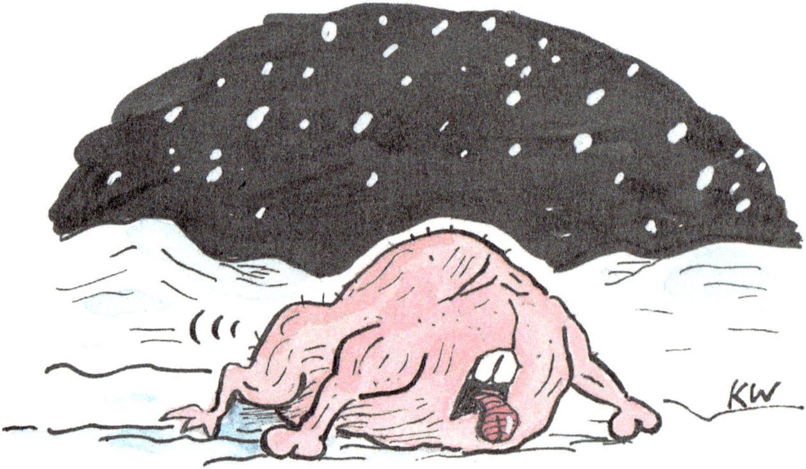
KW

'Stuffing . . . stuffing . . .'

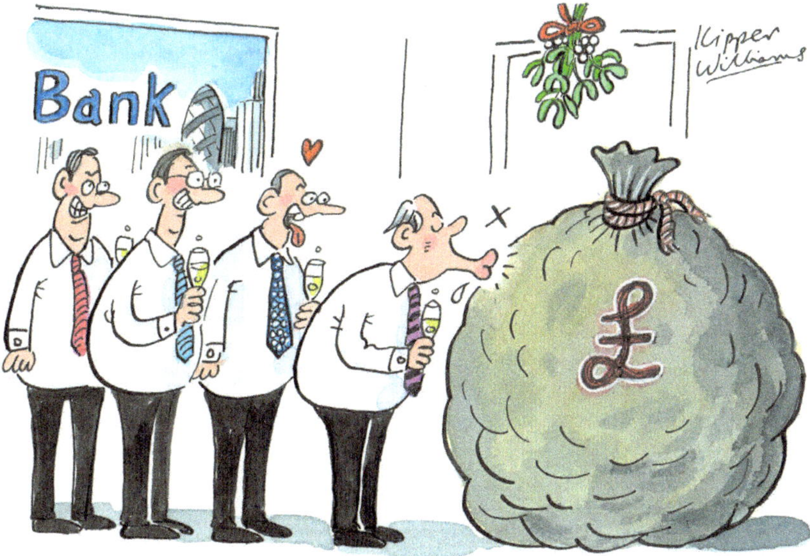
Bank
£
Kipper Williams

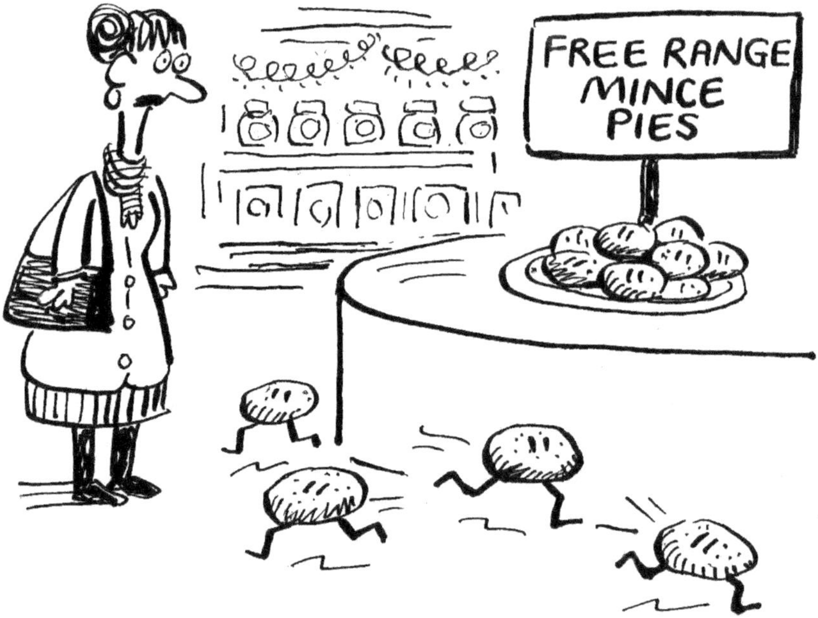
FREE RANGE
MINCE
PIES

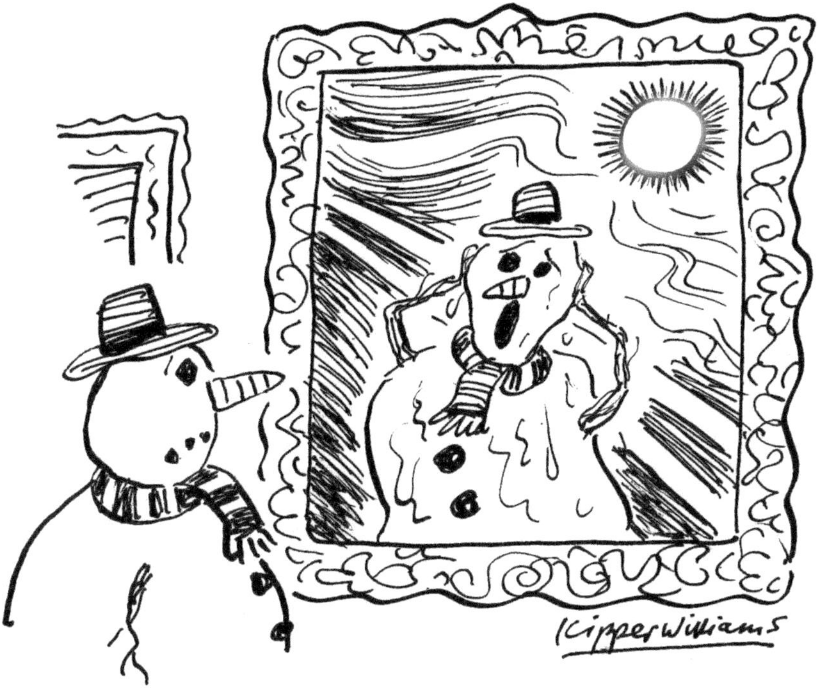
KipperWilliams

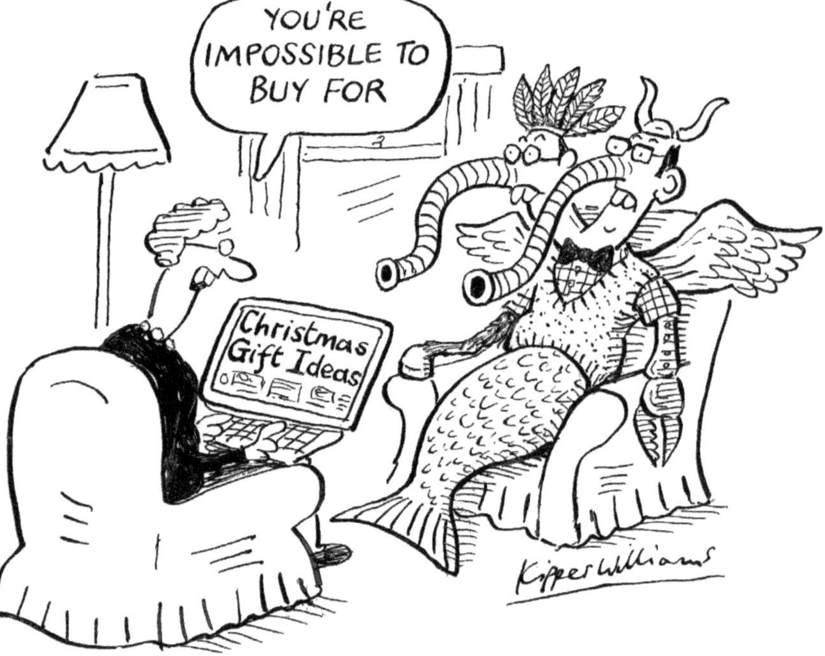
YOU'RE IMPOSSIBLE TO BUY FOR
Christmas Gift Ideas
Kipper Williams

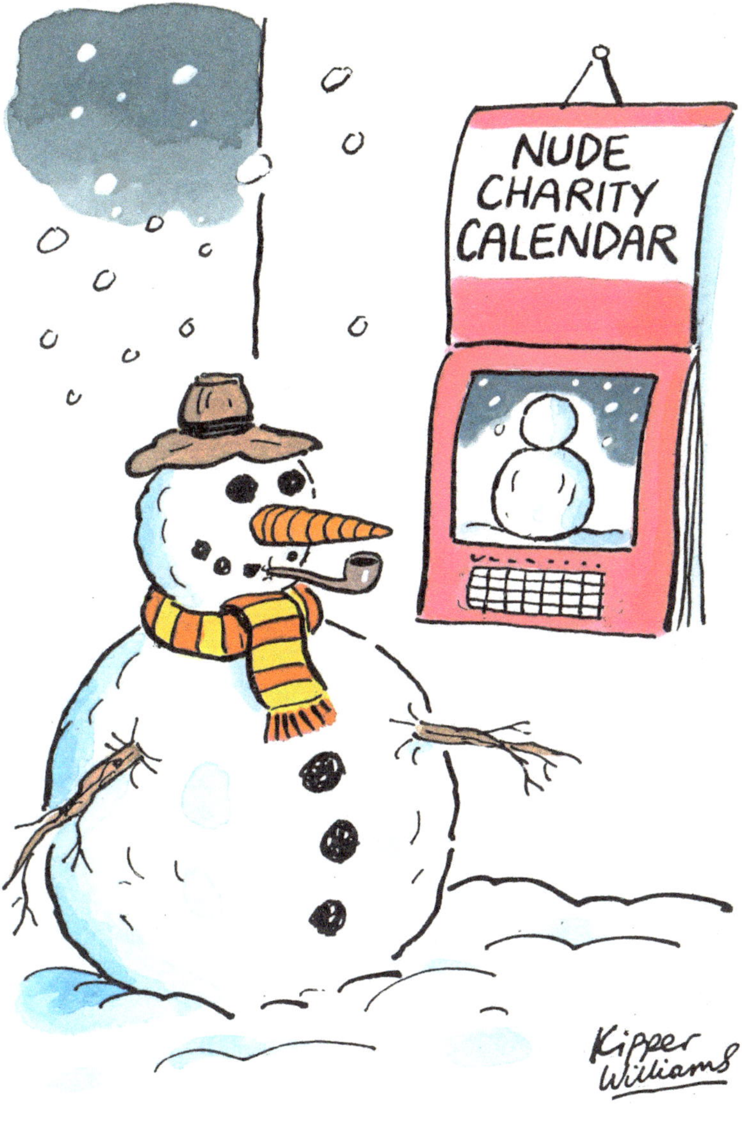
NUDE
CHARITY
CALENDAR
Kipper Williams

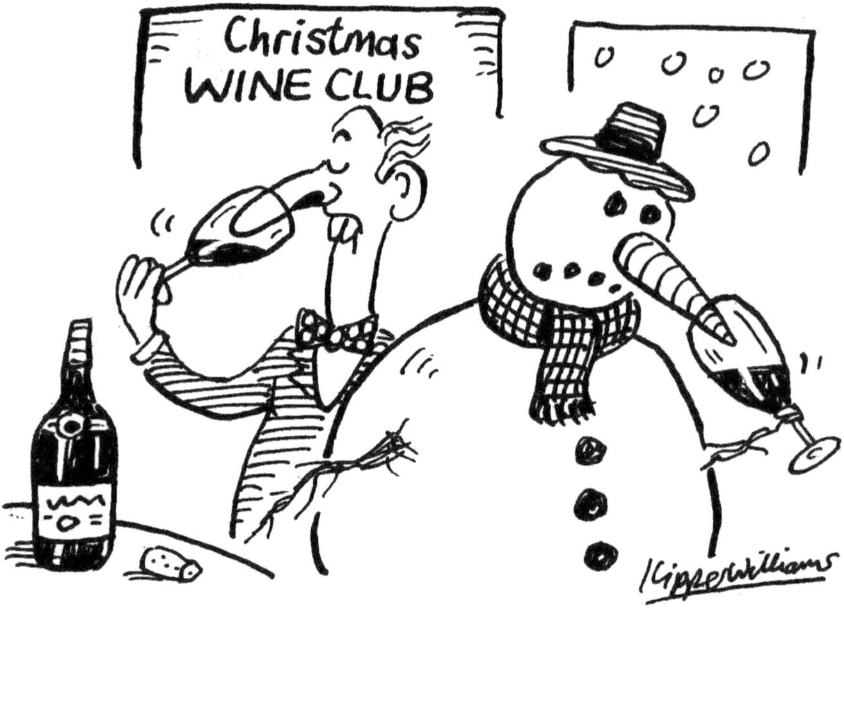
Christmas
WINE CLUB
KipperWilliams

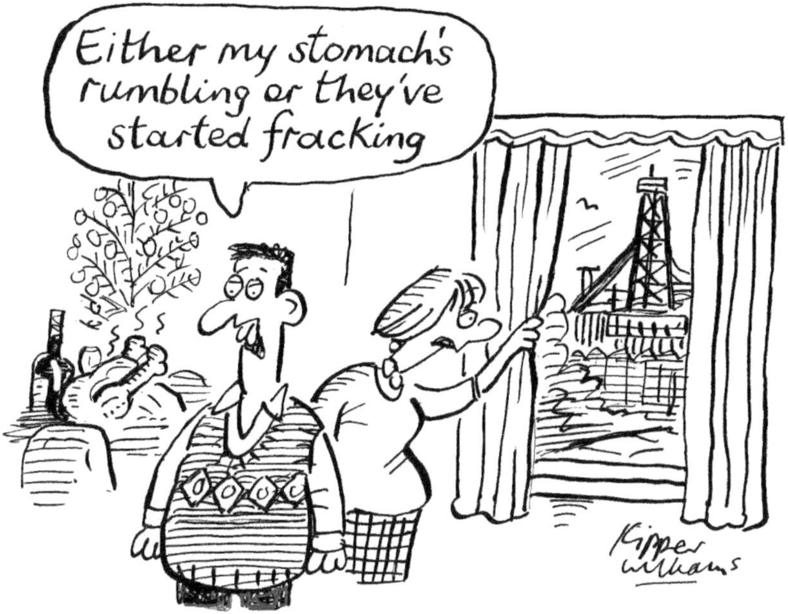
Either my stomach's rumbling or they've started fracking
Kipper Williams

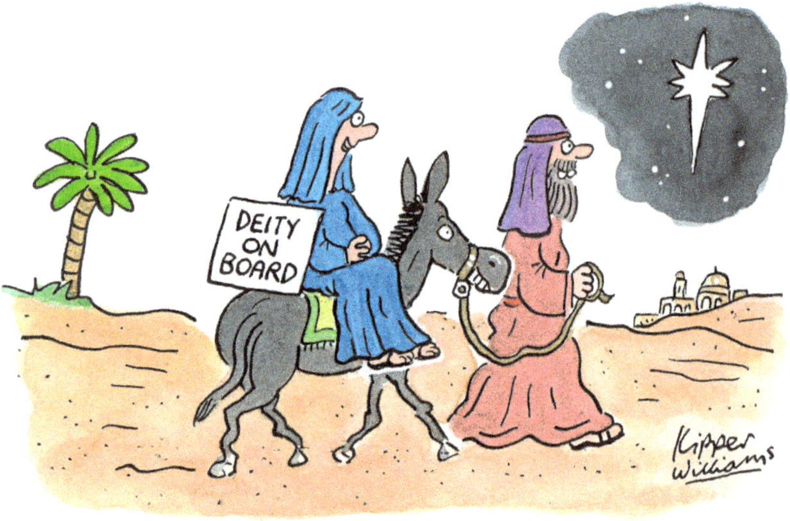
DEITY
ON
BOARD
Kipper
Williams

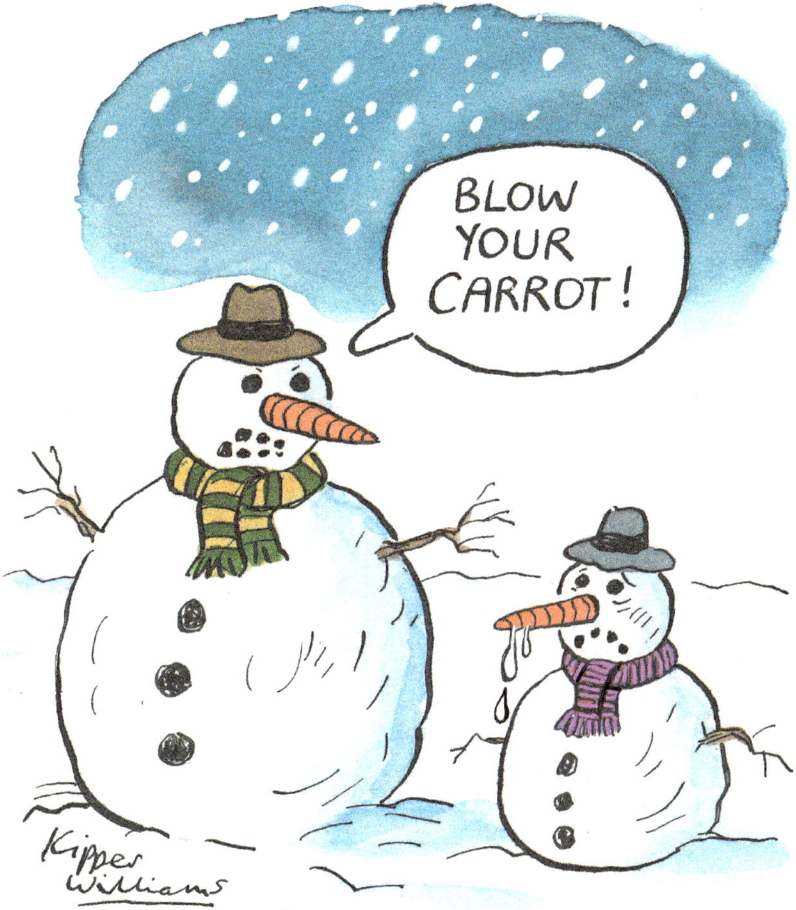
BLOW
YOUR
CARROT!
Kipper
Williams

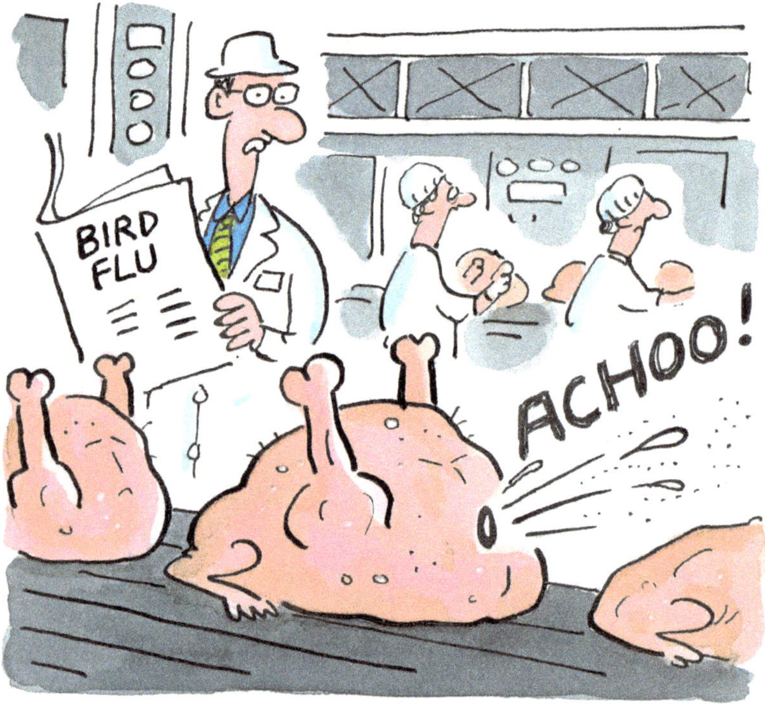
BIRD FLU
ACHOO!

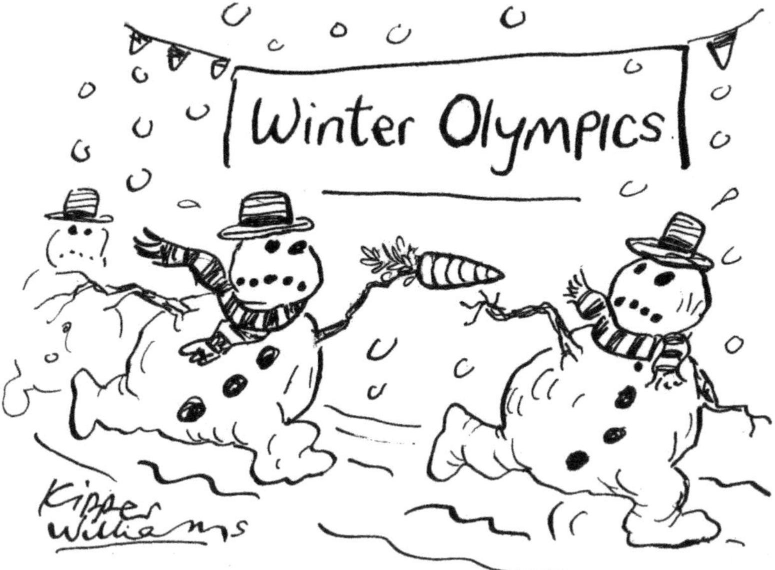
Winter Olympics
Kipper Williams

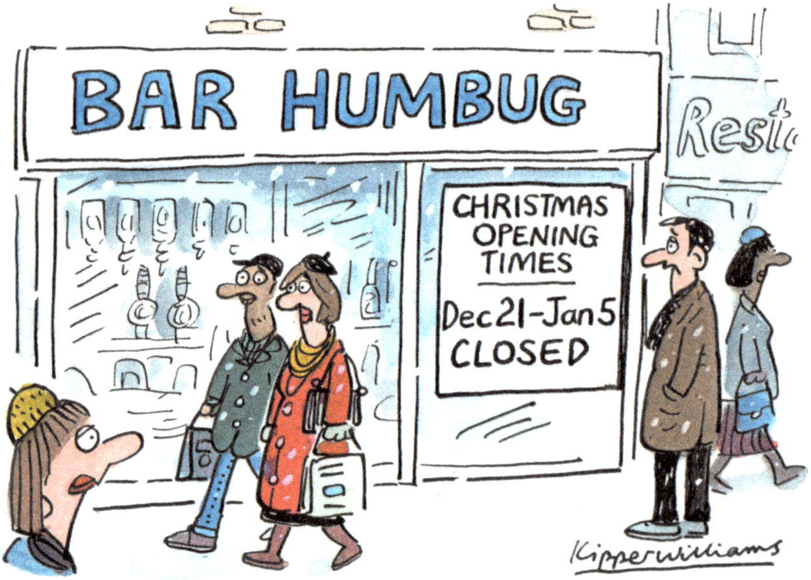
BAR HUMBUG
CHRISTMAS OPENING TIMES
Dec21-Jan5 CLOSED
Kipperwilliams

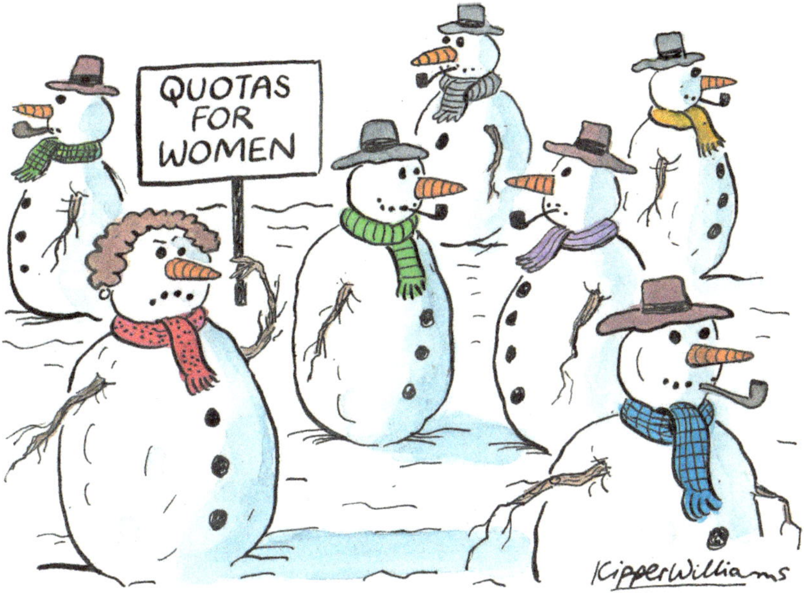
QUOTAS FOR WOMEN
KipperWilliams

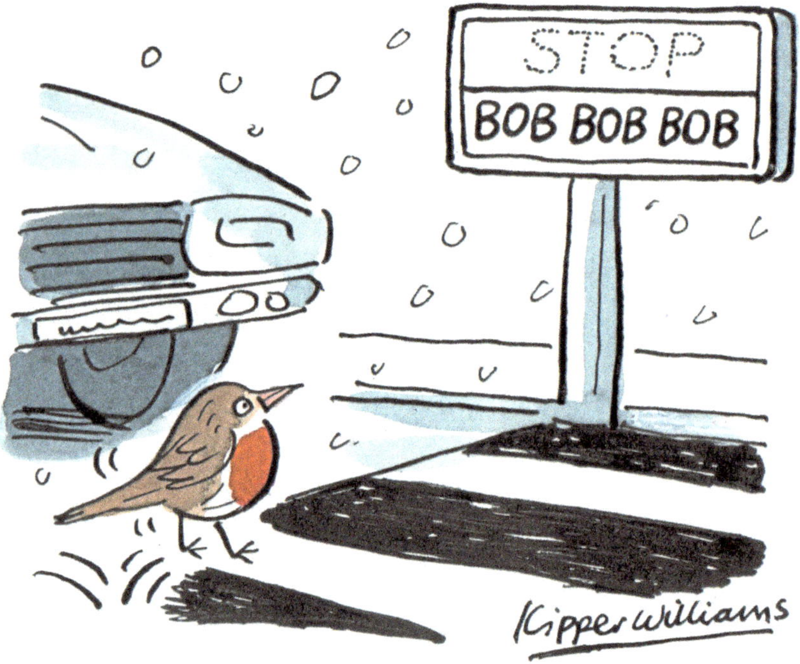
STOP
BOB BOB BOB
Kipper Williams

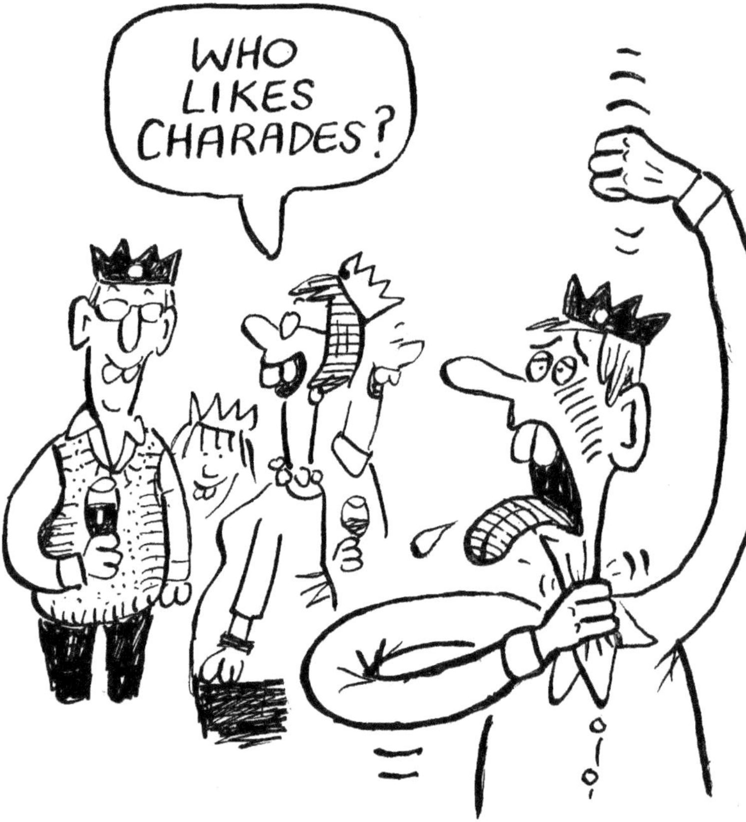
WHO LIKES CHARADES?

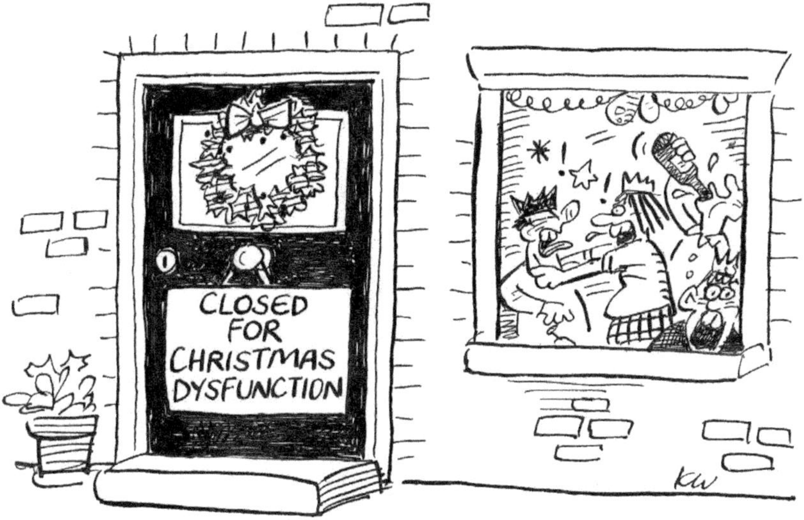
CLOSED
FOR
CHRISTMAS
DYSFUNCTION
KW

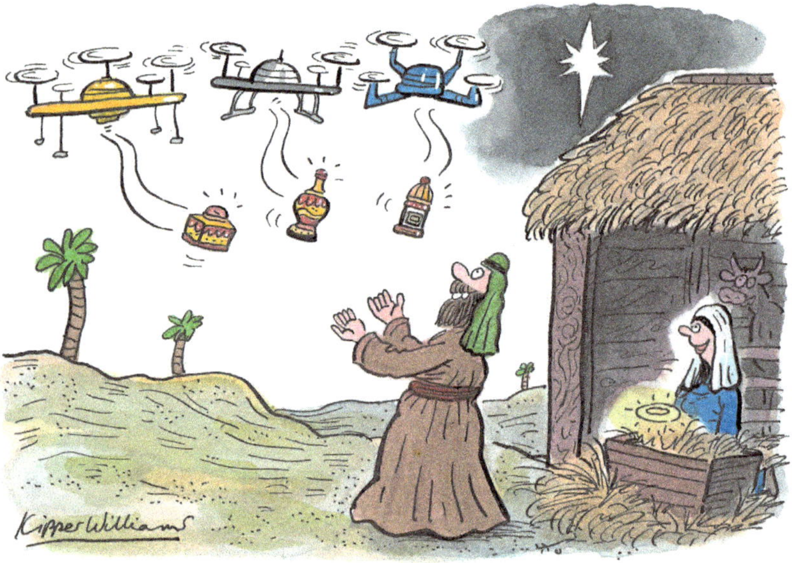
Kipper Williams

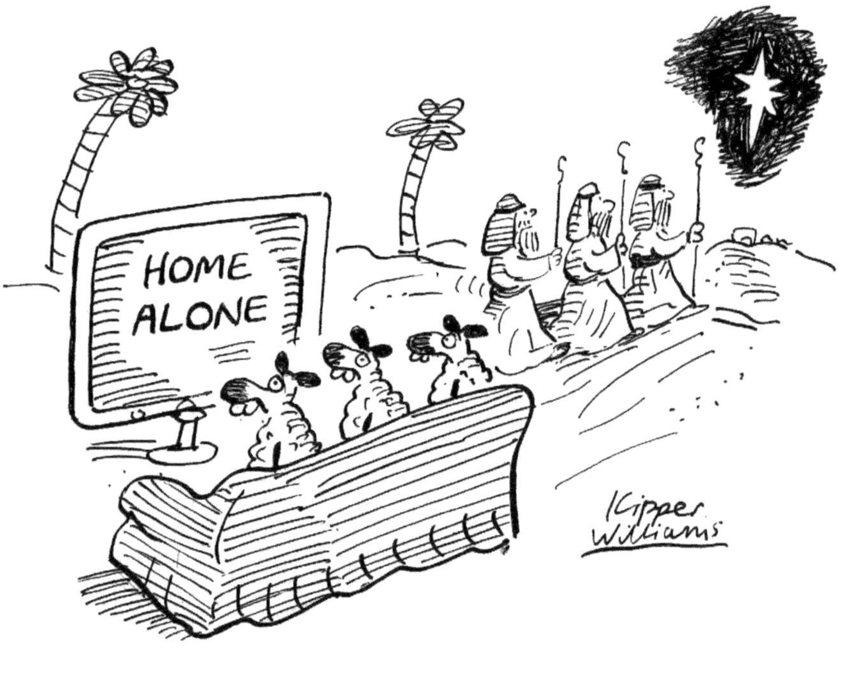
HOME
ALONE
Kipper
Williams

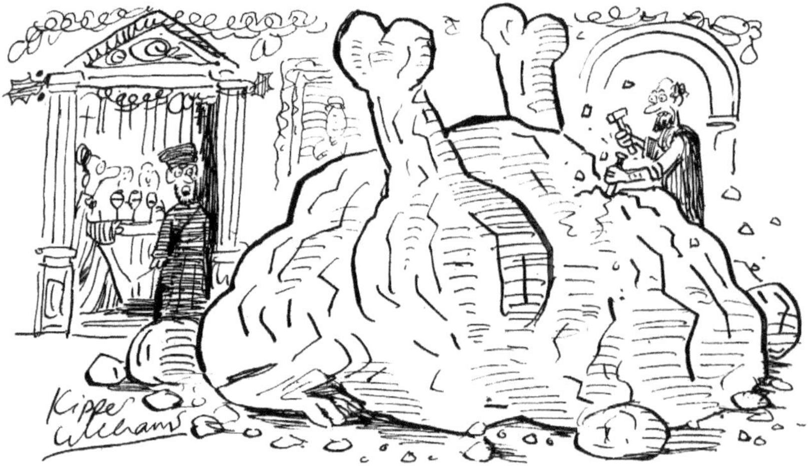
Kipper Williams

'Michelangelo, when I asked you to carve…'

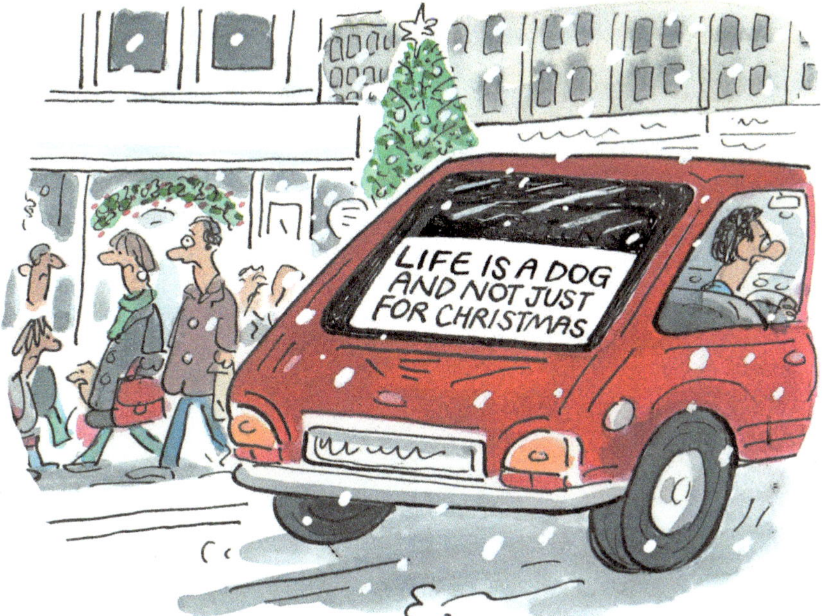
LIFE IS A DOG AND NOT JUST FOR CHRISTMAS

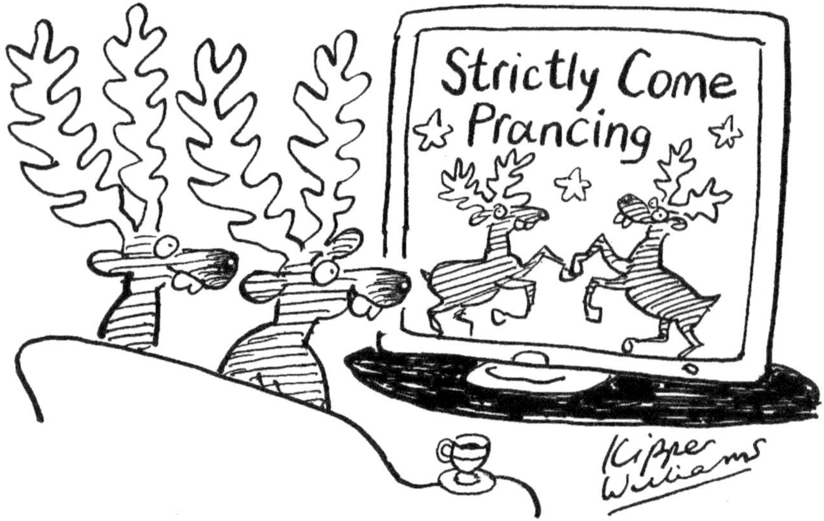
Strictly Come Prancing
Kipper Williams